A Friend in Need

SONJA MASSIE

SIGNAL HILL™

PUBLICATIONS

This book is fiction. The author invented the names, people, places, and events. If any of them are like real places, events, or people (living or dead), it is by chance.

SIGNAL HILL™

PUBLICATIONS

Copyright © 1997
Signal Hill Publications
An imprint of New Readers Press
U.S. publishing division of Laubach Literacy International
Box 131, Syracuse, New York 13210-0131

Printed in the United States of America

Illustration by Patricia A. Rapple
Original cover art by Gary Gray

9 8 7 6 5 4 3 2 1

Library of Congress Cataloging-in-Publication Data

Massie, Sonja.

A friend in need / Sonja Massie.

p. cm. — (Janet Dailey's love scenes)

ISBN 1-56853-028-5 (pbk.)
1. Readers for new literates. 2. Readers—Love stories.
I. Title. II. Series: Dailey, Janet. Janet Dailey's love
scenes.

PE1126.A4M376   1997
428.6'2—dc20   96-36729
                                          CIP

Chapter 1

"Hey! What are you doing in my tree?" Clay Davis stood under the big old almond tree in his front yard. All he could see was a pair of legs sticking out from the leaves. He couldn't see the person's face. But he or she was wearing faded blue jeans and a pair of small, grubby sneakers.

He walked closer to the tree. Grabbing a limb, he shook it. "Hey, you!" he yelled again. "What's going on here?"

The person would never hear him—it sounded as if a chain saw was running up there. He shook the limb harder.

Suddenly, branches, twigs, and leaves crashed to the lawn at his feet. One limb nearly hit his head on the way down.

The chain saw sputtered, then stopped. A cloud of blue smoke floated down to him. The oily smell filled his lungs, and he coughed.

A head popped out of the leaves. It wore a crown of flaming red curls. The face frowned down at him. Coffee brown eyes flashed.

"Look out below!" a female voice shouted. "Didn't anyone ever tell you not to stand under a tree that's being pruned?"

Clay smiled in spite of himself. It had been a long time since he had seen a face that pretty. In fact, he wasn't sure he ever had. It was heart-shaped with freckles sprinkled across the nose.

"Is that right?" he asked, grinning up at her. "Well, someone should have told you not to go climbing around in other people's trees."

She gave him a tired sigh and shook her head. "I have to climb around in your tree," she said. "How else am I going to prune it for you?"

"Prune it?" he asked. "Why would you think I want you to prune it?"

The woman looked up at the sky and rolled her eyes. "Mr. Moore," she said, "you called me yesterday. You asked me to come over and prune the almond tree in your front yard. If you don't like the way I'm doing it, just say so."

His grin widened. "My name is Clay Davis," he said. "And I have no idea what you're talking about."

"But . . . but . . ." she stammered. Her eyes searched for the mailbox. It was at the end of the brick driveway. "This is

375 Ashwood Avenue," she said. "And this is the only almond tree in the front yard."

Clay shook his head slowly. His blue eyes twinkled with amusement. "This is 375 *North* Ashwood Avenue. You blew it, lady."

Her frown quickly turned to a blush. "Uh-oh."

She pulled back into the leaves. Clay watched as the scruffy sneakers searched for footholds on the trunk.

She climbed down from the tree. First, Clay saw more blue-jeaned leg. Then a slender, but shapely, figure. The chain saw dangled from her gloved hand.

As she climbed down, Clay moved toward her. He meant to take the saw from her, like a gentleman. He reached out.

But his hands seemed to have a mind of their own. Instead of taking the saw, they closed around her small waist.

He lowered her to the ground. Then he stood, quietly looking down at her. She blushed more deeply. The flush added even more color to her already pink cheeks.

"I'm . . . I'm really sorry," she said. "I don't know what to say." She looked down at the pile of branches and twigs at their feet. With a shrug, she said, "I could try to graft them back on but . . ." Her voice trailed away to a whisper.

"Well, it needed pruning anyway," he said. She felt bad enough. It was time to let her off the hook. "Go ahead and finish the job," he added. "I'll pay you whatever you were going to charge Mr. Moore."

She lifted her chin proudly. "I'll finish the pruning," she said. "But I won't charge you. It wouldn't be right. You didn't ask for the service."

Clay turned and looked at the old Ford pickup in the driveway. It was at least 20 years old. And it showed its age. On the dented door were the words:

 S. Brandon
Landscaping

One look at the truck told him she could use the money. But her eyes dared him to press the point.

"OK, have it your way," he said. "But somewhere there's a Mr. Moore waiting. And he *does* intend to pay you. Go prune *his* almond tree. You can come back here this afternoon and finish mine."

She frowned. He could see that she was deciding between pride and need. Need won. "All right," she said. "If you're sure you don't mind." She climbed into the old pickup. "But I'll be back. Just as soon as I finish."

Clay watched until she disappeared at the end of the road. Looking at his watch, he groaned. He'd be late for his board meeting.

So what? Suddenly, it didn't seem so important anymore.

He walked slowly up the sidewalk to his house. Ranch style. Five bedrooms. Tennis court. Pool. It was a beautiful home. "An *executive* home," the real estate agent had said. But he couldn't remember the last time he had company here. It was as empty as Clay Davis's executive life.

He thought of the young woman, her coffee-colored eyes, her red curls. His step quickened. He'd better hurry and get to the office. There was a lot to do before he could leave this afternoon. He had just decided to leave early.

He had to be home when she returned. He had to make sure she didn't ruin his tree. Clay had always liked that almond tree. But never quite as much as today.

Chapter 2

Six hours later Kelly Brandon returned to 375 North Ashwood. She pulled into the brick driveway and turned the key. The old truck's engine rattled to a stop.

Kelly pulled on her work gloves, feeling more tired than she had in weeks. Even more than tired, she was embarrassed. She blushed just thinking about Mr. Davis and his darned almond tree.

For seven years she had been in the landscape business. Pruning the wrong tree was the stupidest mistake she had ever made.

Seven years ago, things had been different. She and her husband, Scott, had been so young. So full of dreams. But their dreams had ended in one tragic moment.

Kelly closed her eyes, remembering the shock, the pain. When she opened them, she saw Mr. Davis at the front door. He walked down the sidewalk to greet her.

He was taller than most men she knew. And he was a lot better looking. She almost smiled, recalling how he had helped her down from the tree. He had towered over her. His eyes had been warm and friendly. His strong hands had felt good at her waist.

For a brief moment, Kelly felt something stir inside her. Feelings seemed to wake deep in her heart and body. Feelings that had been asleep since Scott's death.

Clay waved and smiled at her. At least he had been nice about her mistake. He could have yelled at her. He could have called the police. Worse, he could have sued her.

That was all she needed now. Her savings account was finally starting to grow. Kelly hated even to think of losing it. That small account meant so much.

"Hi," she called to him. She climbed out of the truck. Walking around to the back, she reached for the chain saw. "I thought you'd still be at work," she said.

He had changed his three-piece gray suit for jeans and a T-shirt. She noted that he looked great in both.

"I left the office early," he replied.

He worked in an office, she thought. Probably a doctor or a lawyer. Not everyone could afford to live in this section of town.

"I thought I should help you with the tree," he said. He pulled on the thick leather gloves he had been holding.

Oh, no, she thought. The last thing she needed was another person in the tree with her. Someone who didn't know what he was doing.

"Thanks, Mr. Davis," she said quickly. "I can do it myself."

He smiled at her again. She felt a pair of butterflies flutter in her stomach. He was very handsome with his blue eyes sparkling. The sun lit the gold in his brown hair.

But, even if he *was* handsome, she didn't want him in the tree with her.

"Really, Mr. Davis," she said, "I prefer to work alone."

He cast a quick look at her bare ring finger.

"Come on," he said. "It might be fun. I haven't climbed a tree since my Tarzan days."

Her frown began to fade. A small smile curled her lips.

"I know how to prune a tree," he added. "I'm the one who usually does it, you know."

"Oh, all right," she replied. "But don't fall or drop a limb on my head."

"The way you nearly dropped one on me this morning?" he teased her.

She ignored his laughter and headed for the tree.

He was set on doing this. She guessed she'd just have to make the best of it.

Chapter 3

The back of the truck was full of branches. Kelly and Clay sat under the almond tree, recovering from their work.

"Well, Mr. Davis," she said as she took off her gloves. She flexed her tired hands. "Your tree looks rather pleased with itself. Don't you think so?"

Clay tilted his head. Looking up at the bare limbs, he said, "Yes . . . I'd say it's glad to have the whole thing over."

He lowered his head and smiled at her. "I can't say that I'm happy to be finished, though," he said. "That's the most fun I've had in ages."

Kelly glanced away. She was uneasy with the look he gave her. She didn't know what bothered her most, the gleam in his eyes or her reaction to it.

In the past three years, she hadn't even looked at a man. Now she was sitting under a tree, talking to one. She couldn't recall when she had felt so aware of being close to a male. She hadn't had time to flirt. And she didn't have time now, either.

With a sniff she said, "Pruning a tree is your idea of fun? You must lead a pretty boring life."

"You're right," he said softly. "I do."

The sadness in his face went straight to her heart. She didn't like her heart's reaction; it skipped a beat. In his eyes she could see that he was lonely. She knew a lot about feeling lonely.

"And how about you, Ms. S. Brandon?" he asked. "Do you lead a boring life?"

"My name is Kelly." Grabbing her gloves and the chain saw, she stood. She wasn't comfortable, talking about personal things with this man. His blue eyes had a wicked sparkle, and his grin seemed dangerous.

"I don't have time to be bored," she added.

Turning, she headed back toward her truck. Clay caught up with her. Taking the chain saw from her, he loaded it in the back of the truck with the leaves and cut branches.

"Leaving so soon?" he asked.

Kelly thought she heard a note of regret in his voice.

"Well, the job is finished," she said simply.

"So it is." He sighed and reached for the wallet in his jeans pocket. "Are you sure you won't let me pay you for . . ."

The look on her face stopped him in the middle of his sentence. He put the wallet back into his pocket.

Folding his arms over his broad chest, he said, "OK, OK."

Then, the corners of his mouth lifted into a smile. "I just had a nice thought," he added. "You won't let me pay you. So, let me make dinner for you."

"Dinner?" she replied. Her breath caught in her throat. It was bad enough, sitting under a tree with him. But *dinner?* She couldn't even think about it. "No! I mean . . . no, thank you. I . . . I . . ."

"Just a simple dinner," he argued. "I'll put some steaks on the grill out back. Please. You did a nice thing for me. I'd like to return the favor. One pruning for one dinner. Then we'll be even."

Kelly grinned. He looked like a kid begging for an ice cream cone at a drug store. She had seen the look many times.

"I'd like to. Really, I would," she said. "But my son is at the baby-sitter's. I have to pick him up and . . ."

"A son?" Clay's smile widened. "You have a boy? That's great. Bring him along."

She cocked her head to one side and studied him. She'd heard that men avoided women with children.

"He's eight years old, and he has a lot of energy. Are you sure?" she asked.

"Of course," he replied. "I like kids. I haven't had any of my own." A shadow of regret crossed his face.

"Well, if you're sure," she said, giving in. "I'll have to shower and change clothes."

His blue eyes flitted over her figure. Again, her heart thumped. She didn't want him to think about her words so carefully.

"Take your time," he said. "I'll be here."

Chapter 4

"Hello. Anybody back there?"

Hearing the voice, Clay squinted through the cloud of smoke. But he couldn't see anything or anyone. As he closed the lid on the barbecue grill, he called, "Yeah! Over here."

The haze cleared. Across the yard he saw Kelly. She was standing there, looking pretty in a bright yellow dress.

Her red curls were pulled back into a ponytail.

Clay saw that she had applied a light touch of makeup. He wondered if she always wore a bit when she wasn't working. After a hard day of landscaping, she might like a feminine touch.

Beside Kelly stood a small boy. He looked freshly scrubbed and uncomfortable in his dress shirt and slacks. Only his battered sneakers looked natural on him.

Clay left the grill and walked over to them. "Well, Ms. Brandon," he said, "you don't look like the red-headed woodpecker who was chain-sawing my tree this morning."

Kelly said nothing, but she smiled shyly.

Clay knelt on one knee beside the boy. The child's copper curls and heart-shaped face were just like his mother's.

"And who's this young fellow with you?" Clay asked.

"This is Scottie," she said proudly. Kelly spoke the words as though she were presenting a royal prince.

She turned to her son. "Scottie," she said. "This is Mr. Davis."

"It's nice to meet you, Scottie," Clay said. "But you can call me Clay. If that's all right with your mom," he added.

The boy looked up at his mother. She nodded.

"I'm glad to meet you, Clay," Scottie said in a grown-up voice for an eight-year-old. He held his hand out to Clay. The man took the small hand in his giant one. Scottie's handshake was as firm as an adult's.

The boy glanced over Clay's shoulder. In a second, his dignity disappeared. His small freckled face lit up, and he ran across the yard.

"Wow!" he shouted. "You've got a pool. And a submarine, too! Is it remote controlled?"

Clay rose from his knee. He watched as the boy hurried to the edge of the pool. Clay noticed that the child limped, dragging his left foot.

From the corner of his eye, Clay saw Kelly watching him. He knew she was waiting for his reaction. He knew better than to show the pity he felt. The emotion welled up in his throat. But he swallowed it and said, "Yes, Scottie, here's the control."

He picked up the remote unit from a lawn chair. Walking over to the child, he placed it in his small hand.

"I don't have any children of my own," Clay told him. "So, there weren't any toys here for kids to play with. I picked this up at a hobby shop this afternoon. Do you like it?"

"Like it?" Scottie beamed. "It's great!"

The boy sat on the edge of the pool. In a few minutes he had mastered the controls. The submarine circled and dove beneath the water. It rose again with "treasure" from the bottom of the pool—red, blue, and yellow plastic rings.

"Gee, Mr. . . . I mean . . . Clay," Scottie said, excited, "this is like playing video games. Only better! Thanks a lot for getting it!"

Clay nodded, happy that his purchase was a success.

He left the boy and walked over to Kelly. She was sitting in a large double swing beside an orange tree.

A frown creased her pretty face. She wasn't as pleased as her son about the submarine.

"You shouldn't have done that," she said as he sat beside her in the swing. She looked down at her hands, folded in her lap. "That's an expensive toy for one evening's play."

Clay tried to listen to what she was saying. But instead, he was thinking about how soft her hands looked. How could they be so delicate, considering the work she did?

They sat several inches apart. Her perfume blended nicely with the scent of the orange blossoms nearby. He could feel the warmth of her bare arm near his.

"Scottie won't be the only one playing with it," he said. "I've always wanted one of those myself. Besides, I don't mind the cost."

"But I do," she said.

He heard the quiet strength in her voice. He saw the proud set of her chin. And he remembered someone else.

Meg, his ex-wife.

She had looked like that when she had told him it was over.

"I'm not happy, Clay," she had said. "You've always taken care of me. I've depended on you . . . too much. I still love you. But I need to take care of myself. I need to know I can."

Five years later, Clay knew what he had done wrong. And he vowed not to make the same mistake with another woman. He thought he had learned his lesson.

But had he? He watched Kelly's son hobble around his pool. Those old feelings began to grow again. He wanted to protect, to make everything better.

"What happened to Scottie's leg?" he asked. He tried to sound casual. But he could hear the pity in his own words.

"He was hurt in a car wreck," she said.

Clay looked at Scottie and felt sick inside. The boy was doing well with the submarine. His hands and fingers worked better than his leg.

Kelly turned to Clay. She swallowed hard and said, "The accident killed my husband. That was three years ago."

Clay recalled the printing on the side of the pickup:

🌲🌲 S. Brandon
Landscaping

"Was your husband a landscaper, too?" he asked.

"Yes." She nodded. "Scott and I started the business together. I've kept it going since his death."

He looked at her with new respect. "You must work hard," he said, "to support yourself and Scottie."

"I pay the monthly bills," she said. He could hear the pride in her voice. "The hard part," she added, "is having enough left over for medical expenses."

"Pretty bad, huh?" Clay could only imagine.

She lowered her voice. Again, she stared down at her folded hands. "Yes, pretty bad. Scottie's had a series of operations to put his leg right."

Clay wondered how much worse the boy's original injuries had been. "Will he need many more operations?"

"One more major surgery. Then he should be able to walk without limping."

"Is it an expensive operation?"

She laughed grimly. "Aren't they all?"

Clay's problem-solving brain shifted into high gear. "How about your insurance?"

She shrugged. "That ran out long ago."

"That's too bad."

She forced a smile. "Don't worry about us. We do OK, really. We just take it a day at a time."

Clay could tell that Kelly wanted to change the subject. But he couldn't resist asking, "How much money do you need?"

Seeing the shocked look on her face, he knew he had blown it. This was none of his business. The question had been rude, but he really wanted to know.

First she stuttered and stammered. Finally, with a bit more coaxing, she told him the amount. It was a lot less than he had expected.

Clay had six savings accounts. Each of them held more than that.

"Heck, Kelly, that isn't so much," he said, hoping to offer her some comfort.

But pain filled her eyes. Clay knew he had said the wrong thing . . . again.

"It's a lot of money," she said softly, "if you don't have it."

"Yes. Of course it is," he mumbled. "I'm sorry, Kelly. I didn't mean to be a jerk."

Her face softened. "You're not being a jerk, Clay. You're a very nice man. And I appreciate your concern. Really, I do. I'm just not comfortable talking about it with you. If you don't mind."

"No, of course not. I understand."

The silence grew heavy between them. The toy submarine hummed. Bees droned in the orange tree behind them. The steaks sizzled on the grill.

Ashamed that he hadn't been more sensitive, Clay stood and walked over to the barbecue. He turned the steaks slowly. He had to fight the urge to offer her the money.

He peered through the smoke at Scottie and thought of his six savings accounts. What was he saving for? A trip to Club Med next winter?

A new boat? He would take it to the lake maybe once a summer.

He could pay for the child's operation. And he'd never even miss the money.

Clay glanced toward Kelly. She was watching him. Again, he noted the set of her chin, the fire in her eyes. He knew better than to offer.

Meg had taught him that lesson. He had learned the hard way. He wouldn't forget so quickly.

With a sigh, Clay gave up the idea.

But he couldn't help wanting to help, *needing* to help.

He glanced around his backyard. The shrubs were overgrown. The flower beds lay empty. Weeds dotted the lawn.

Clay smiled. There was more than one way to put money into her pockets. And this plan was even better than the first.

It would make sure that he could see Kelly again . . . and again . . . and again.

Chapter 5

Kelly tossed her hand shovel into the bed of marigolds. She wiped the sweat from her brow and said, "You know . . . you aren't fooling me, Clay. It's pretty clear what you're doing."

Clay's eyes opened wide. He gave her his best innocent look. "What are you talking about?" he asked, taking a packet of seeds from his pocket.

"Don't give me that look," she said. "Scottie puts on the same one, just before I ground him."

"Why, Ms. Brandon, I have no idea what you mean," he replied.

She stood and brushed the dirt off her knees. "You do too. For the last two months, you've been making up things to do in this yard. This is now the best tended piece of land in the city."

Waving a hand at the flower beds and neatly trimmed shrubs, she said, "City Hall doesn't look this good."

He stood, too. Looking at her, he wondered if Kelly knew how pretty she was. Her red hair was waving in the wind. Her freckled nose had a dab of yellow daylily pollen on it. He longed to reach out and brush it away.

For eight weeks he had kept himself from touching her. It was getting more and more difficult not to.

He shrugged. "I like having a nice yard," he said.

Slowly, she shook her head. "That isn't it. And we both know it."

"Then what is it?" he asked, afraid of her answer.

"You're just trying to be nice," she snapped.

He laughed. "Well. The nerve of me. I should be shot at sunrise!"

She didn't return his laughter. "You know what I mean," she said. "It isn't right for you to be giving me money."

This time, he was the one to scowl. "What the heck are you saying? I haven't been *giving* you money. You've done a great job here." He nodded toward his new grape arbor and herb garden. "I had a crummy back yard. Now it's a work of art. I'm really happy with your work. You've earned every penny I've paid you."

"We aren't talking about pennies," she said. "This is running into a lot of money."

She stepped closer to him, filling his senses. When she laid her hand on his arm, he felt his heart race.

"Clay," she said softly, "I know why you're doing this. And I'm very thankful. You're a nice man. Scottie and I have grown really fond of you. But . . ."

"But?" he asked. This was it, he thought. She was about to say good-bye. He'd never see her or her shining hair again.

"But," she said, "I can't go on taking advantage of you this way."

She reached up and stroked his cheek. His self-control vanished.

He pulled her to him and pressed his lips to hers. The kiss she gave him was warm and loving. Her arms stole around his neck. Her fingers sifted lightly through his hair.

Finally, he broke the kiss. Burying his face in her soft curls, he said, "I . . . I care for you, Kelly." He kissed her temple. "I care a lot."

She looked up at him. Her eyes were shining. "Me, too," she replied.

"Then let me help you." His hands moved up to cup her face.

"What?" she asked. She looked confused.

"Let me just give you the money," he replied. He brushed a soft curl out of her eyes. "It's nothing to me. You need it for Scottie."

"Clay," she said, "I thought you understood. I can't take money from you." She pulled away from him.

It was his turn to be confused. "Why not?" he asked.

"Because Scottie is *my* child," she said. "*I'll* provide for him. I don't need your charity."

"Charity?" His temper rose. "Is that what you call it? I thought it was a friend offering help. It's great to be independent, Kelly. But you can be too proud. The most important thing is what's best for your child."

Tears filled her eyes. They spilled onto her cheeks. "How can you understand?" she said. "You have all this . . ."

She waved her hand toward the house, the pool, the Mercedes. "And what do I have? Two things. My son, and the pride I take in providing for him."

She began to cry even harder. Clay wanted to take her in his arms again. But he didn't think it would be a good idea.

"Damn you, Clay Davis," she said through her sobs. "You're making me choose between the only two things in my life that matter."

A moment later, she was gone. Clay was left, standing alone in the middle of his perfect lawn.

He stood there for a long time. He cursed the day they had met. He cursed the almond tree.

But mostly, Clay cursed himself.

Chapter 6

Kelly walked through her front door, feeling tired and sick. She wanted to forget what Clay had said. She wanted to ignore his offer. But she couldn't get it out of her mind.

Scottie sat in front of the TV playing video games. Lately, he had been playing them a lot more often. Kelly worried about him. She hadn't seen his friends around as much as usual.

"Why aren't you outside playing?" she asked.

She sat on the floor beside him and picked up the other remote.

He shrugged his frail shoulders. "Don't want to," he replied.

Kelly began to play against him. Together they guided the tiny figures across the screen. They jumped over gooey black tar pits and ran from slimy green monsters. Finally, they climbed the castle wall and rescued the princess from the wicked witch.

"Why do we have to save the princess?" she asked her son. "Why can't she just climb out herself?"

"Because she'd rather get rescued," he replied matter-of-factly. "It's easier to let the prince do it."

Kelly lifted one eyebrow. "Oh really? Well, I think that stinks."

"Why?" he asked.

"Because *I* wouldn't want to sit around and wait for some prince to come along," she said firmly. "What if he took forever? What if his horse got a flat tire?"

"Mom!" Scottie looked shocked at her ignorance. "Horses don't have tires!"

"So, what if his armor rusted in a rainstorm?" she said, punching his shoulder playfully. "What if he saw the dragon and chickened out all of a sudden? I could be sitting there for years, waiting. I'd want to get on with my life."

"Yeah, but you're not like most girls," he said with great authority. "Most of them would want a prince to save them."

"Don't bet on it, kiddo." She stood and put her remote away.

Changing the subject, she asked about Scottie's friends.

"I haven't seen Pete or Mike much lately," she said as she walked over to the sofa and sat down.

Scottie suddenly looked sad. He turned his back to her and began to play again.

"Where have they been?" she asked, pressing the point.

"We don't hang out much anymore." He stuck out his bottom lip in a pout.

"Why not?" she asked. So . . . this was why he was spending so much time alone.

"Cause I can't be part of their stupid club."

Kelly watched his face closely. "Why not?"

Tears welled up in his eyes. He brushed them away angrily with his sleeve. He stared at the TV and kept on playing. "They don't have the club meetings at the park anymore," he said with a sniff.

"Where do they have them?"

"In Pete's new tree house," he replied. The drops spilled down his face.

Kelly didn't have to ask any more questions. She knew the answer to her son's loneliness. It was simple. He couldn't climb the tree, so he wasn't in the club.

Kids could be so cruel.

"I'm sorry, Scottie," she said.

He sniffed loudly. "No big deal," he replied, still staring at the TV screen.

It *was* a big deal. That was as clear as the tears on his face. But Scottie was a lot like her. He didn't admit his pain. He held it inside and acted as though everything was fine.

Kelly wished she hadn't passed that trait on to her son. She was proud and strong and brave. She would never allow any prince to rescue *her*. It was a lonely way to live. Some days Kelly felt like she had been living in that empty tower for a long, long time.

Chapter 7

"Meg, what's wrong with trying to take care of another person?" Clay asked.

He sat across the table from his ex-wife. Before them lay several years' tax records. An hour ago, she had asked him to come to her apartment. And he had come willingly.

Clay was at ease with Meg. The romance between them was over, and they were still good friends. Clay was thankful. She was a smart woman, and he would always be glad to have her in his life. Their marriage just hadn't worked out. They had been much too young at the time.

"I've always wanted to help," he said, staring down at his coffee cup. "I wanted to help you. Now I want to help Kelly and Scottie. What's wrong with that?"

Meg took a sip from her cup. "I guess it depends on why you want to help," she said.

"Why? What does that have to do with anything?" Clay was more confused than ever. But then, he felt he was always confused when it came to women.

"It has everything to do with it," she replied. "Sometimes, we help because we love someone or because we want them to love us. Sometimes, we don't feel in control of our own lives. So we think we'll feel better if we take control of someone else's."

She looked up at him with sadness in her eyes. "Usually, we think we know what's best for the other person. And, of course, we can't know. We aren't living *their* life."

Clay thought for a long moment. He didn't want to admit she was right. But her words did have a ring of truth to them. He wanted to think he offered help out of love. And often he did. He had to wonder how often he did it for the other reasons.

"Is that what I did to you, Meg?" he asked, not wanting to hear her answer.

She simply nodded.

"I'm sorry. I did try to take control of your life. I thought I knew what was best about your work, your schooling. Thinking back, I remember giving you a lot of bad advice."

"Not all of it was bad, Clay," she said. "Many times you were right. But some things I wanted to do myself. Even if I did them wrong. I wanted to learn on my own, make my own mistakes. Then, if I had a victory, it was mine. I needed those victories to feel whole."

"And I took that away from you," he said sadly.

He thought of Kelly and what she had said that afternoon. She was so proud of taking care of her son.

And he had tried to take control. He had acted as if he could do it better than she could. No wonder she had been so hurt and angry.

"You didn't take anything from me, Clay," Meg said. She poured him a fresh cup of coffee. "No one can *take* your power from you. You have to give it away, like I did."

"But I didn't make it very easy for you to keep it," he said.

She laughed and nodded. "That's true. Very true." Her eyes softened. "But you're learning, Clay. And in the end, that's all that counts."

Clay remembered Kelly's sad eyes and the last words she had said to him. *You're making me choose between the only two things in my life that matter.*

He hoped Meg was right. This time, he *really* hoped she was right.

Chapter 8

A few nights later, Kelly lay alone in her big bed. In one hand she held an empty cup; in the other, a half-read novel. Even with a cup of cocoa and a good book, she couldn't get to sleep.

She turned out the lights. With a sigh she snuggled deeper between the sheets. In the darkness, her worries closed around her. She felt as though she couldn't breathe under their weight.

Sitting up in bed, she turned the lamp back on.

Only 10 minutes before, she had told Scottie not to be afraid of the dark. He was sure a "swamp monster" would eat him alive every time his lights were turned out. Someday soon, Scottie would outgrow his fears. Would she ever be rid of hers?

Kelly tilted the cup and drank the last cold drop of cocoa. She couldn't stop thinking about Scottie.

This afternoon, he had come home with a gash on his head. Both of his knees had been scraped. He had tried to climb the tree and join his friends in the tree house. Unable to get a firm footing, he had fallen.

Kelly was sure that somehow it was her fault. She hadn't been able to save the money fast enough.

Three years had passed since Scott had died. Three years of Scottie's boyhood.

He needed to be able to walk without limping. He needed to be able to run and climb trees with his friends. And he needed to do those things *now*, not when she had finally scraped the money together.

Clay Davis had been right. She *was* too proud. Much too proud. She was putting her own ego before her child's welfare.

Or was she?

Kelly closed her eyes and thought about Clay. He really was a good man. He just wanted to help. His offer had been made in kindness. Why had she refused it?

Kelly knew the answer. And she knew it had nothing to do with pride. She didn't want to need Clay. Kelly didn't want to need *anyone*.

She thought of her own childhood. Of her mother kissing her good-bye ... and never coming home again. Of all the foster homes.

When Kelly had been 16, she had met Scott. He had been her hero, giving her all the love her heart could hold.

But Scott had left her, too. Just like the others.

Kelly wanted to love Clay Davis. She wanted to take the risk and admit that she already did. But she was afraid. As afraid as Scottie was of his swamp monster.

Swamp monsters never hurt anyone, except in the movies. They never left you to cry alone in your bed at three in the morning.

But love hurt. It was all a big game. And it always hurt so badly when you lost.

Kelly knew that lesson better than most.

She turned out the light again, knowing the old ghost of loneliness would return. He wasn't a pleasant bed partner. But he was certainly a faithful one.

Chapter 9

Clay's heart jumped when he heard the voice on the phone. It was Kelly, calling him at work. That must mean . . . ?

He didn't know what it meant. Surely, she wouldn't call him at work just to yell at him again. Kelly was too polite for that.

"Yes, Kelly?" he said hopefully.

"I'll take it," she replied.

His joy faded. Her voice was different. The sparkle was gone. She sounded tired and beaten.

"Did you hear me, Clay?" she said. "I'll take the money." She paused, then added, "If the offer still stands, that is."

He sank into his leather chair and leaned his elbows on his desk. After asking his secretary to leave, he said, "Kelly I'm glad you called. I'm so sorry for what I said. Will you forgive me?"

At first she didn't reply. He thought that she hadn't heard him. Then she said quietly, "Is the offer still open?"

"No," he replied in a soft voice. "As a matter of fact, it isn't."

He heard her catch her breath. The sound went straight to his heart.

"Clay," she said, "you were right. I was a fool to deny Scottie this chance."

He leaned back in his chair and shook his head. "You're many things, Kelly," he said. "You're a great mother, a beautiful woman, and a heck of a landscaper. But you're not a fool. You don't need my money. And whether I want to admit it or not, you don't need me." He paused to draw a deep breath. "There's a way you can pay for Scottie's operation yourself. Every single cent of it. Right away."

Again there was a long silence. "How?" she asked. Her voice was shaking.

"I have a friend by the name of Mark Steeple. He dropped by my house the other day. He was very impressed with the job you did on my yard. He's building a new home down the street from me. I hope you don't mind that I gave him your number. He has three acres that will need landscaping."

"Do you mean *Doctor* Mark Steeple? The surgeon?"

"That's him."

"I've heard of him," she said. Clay could hear the hope in her voice. "He's very good."

"He's the best." Clay laughed. "But don't tell him I said so. He's a big enough snob already."

She didn't reply, but he thought he could hear her sniff.

"You have enough saved to cover the hospital bill," he said. "I told Mark about Scottie's problem. He said he'd be glad to work out a trade with you."

This time he was sure he heard her sniff. "Are you crying, Kelly?" he asked softly. Another sniff. "Please don't cry."

After a long silence, she said, "You were wrong, you know."

"Yes, I was," he admitted. "I never should have . . ."

"No, not that." She paused. "You were wrong about us not needing you. Scottie is going to be scared when he has the operation. I will be, too."

Clay relaxed his grip on the phone. He smiled, feeling better than he had in days. "I'll be there, Kelly," he said. "I'll be there for Scottie *and* for you."

Chapter 10

Looking around Dr. Mark Steeple's backyard, Kelly felt a wave of pride wash over her. In less than a year, she had turned three acres of bare ground into a fairyland.

Stone walkways led through the English cottage garden. Red roses climbed snowy white lattices. The air was sweet with the scent of lavender and other fragrant herbs. A waterfall trickled into a shaded pool of water lilies surrounded by velvet brown cattails.

Kelly had done a great job, and she knew it. The entire town seemed to know it. Already, she had received enough calls to keep her busy for months.

Hearing footsteps behind her, she turned and saw Clay coming down the walk. Her pulse quickened at the sight of him. He was dressed in khakis and a golf shirt, his usual Saturday attire. He and Mark Steeple often played a few rounds on the weekends.

"Good morning, gorgeous," he said as he took her in his arms and kissed her. "Mark told me I'd find you out here, admiring your handiwork."

Her arms curled around his neck as she snuggled into his embrace. Day by day, this gentle man was winning her over. Moment by moment, she was finding it easier to trust her heart to his keeping. If only they could get through the next few weeks. Maybe then . . .

No, she couldn't think that far. She couldn't think beyond next Monday morning.

"I came over to check the pump on the waterfall," she said. "And I thought I'd have a quiet moment, communing with nature."

He released her and stood back, studying her face. "Am I interrupting your . . . meditation?"

She shook her head. "No, of course not. You may interrupt me any time at all."

Taking her hand, he led her over to a teak bench. They sat side by side, enjoying the soothing sounds of the waterfall.

In a moment of weakness—or was it strength?—Kelly leaned her head on Clay's shoulder.

"Clay, I'm so worried," she said.

He slipped his arm around her waist and pulled her close. "I know. Me, too. But Mark is an excellent surgeon."

Hot tears flooded Kelly's eyes. Fear caused her throat to constrict. "Even he says it's a long, difficult surgery."

Looking into Clay's face, she could see his fear. In the past months, he had grown to love Scottie, too.

"Like you told me once," he said, "we'll just take it a day at a time." He pressed a kiss to her forehead. "And if we need to . . . an hour or a minute at a time."

For what seemed like forever, Kelly and Clay had sat in the hospital waiting room. The pale blue decor was no doubt supposed to have a calming effect on visitors. But nothing helped Kelly's worries. Not even Clay's words of support.

"It's been over eight hours now," she said, tearing a pinch of Styrofoam off the empty cup in her hand. "They said it would take six or seven."

"I'm sure it must be hard to predict things like this."

"Or maybe something's wrong."

"I'm sure everything's fine." Clay's smile was gentle and reassuring. But Kelly could hear the concern in his voice.

At the other end of the room, the door swung open. Dr. Mark Steeple walked toward them. He looked worn out.

Kelly searched his face. But she couldn't read his blank expression. She couldn't tell if her son's surgery had been successful. She couldn't even tell if he had survived.

Heart pounding, Kelly jumped to her feet and hurried toward the doctor.

And, as he had promised, Clay was beside her, ready to share in whatever the outcome might be.

Chapter 11

"Do you, Clay, take Kelly as your lawfully wedded wife . . . ?"

For two years, Clay Davis had imagined this day. In the past few months, he had played the moment over and over in his mind.

He had thought he might be nervous. And he was.

And he had thought he might be uncertain. He wasn't.

Not at all.

After repeating his vows, he listened as Kelly said hers. In her eyes he saw only love. Like him, she seemed certain.

Standing in Mark Steeple's garden, Clay and Kelly shared their vows before friends and family. The California sun shone warm on their faces. Clay couldn't recall a more perfect day.

Then, the minister said, "Now I would like to include another member of this new family in the vows."

Everyone turned to Scottie, who was standing quietly behind his mother. The 10-year-old's legs were strong now, his confidence level high. Clay thought of the hours they had spent together in the pool. The exercise. The physical therapy that had healed more than just an injured limb. For both of them.

"Scott," the minister said, "do you give your blessing to this union?"

Scottie nodded eagerly. A big smile lit his face. "I do!"

"By the power vested in me by the state of California . . . I pronounce you husband, and wife, and son. Clay, you may kiss the bride."

Clay took his time, savoring the moment, too happy to believe it was real. Kelly melted into his arms. She *felt* real, more real than anything in his life had ever felt.

Several of their guests clapped. Scottie giggled. Clay gave Kelly an extra peck on her freckled nose for good luck.

Clay felt a tugging at his sleeve. He looked down to see Scottie beaming up at him. "So, are we a family yet?" the boy asked.

Kelly reached down and squeezed her son's shoulders. "What do *you* think?" she asked him.

"Feels like a family to me," he replied.

"To me, too," Clay added as he folded them into a big, three-way hug. "That's *exactly* what it feels like to me."